GOD'S HEALING FOR THE REJECTED SOUL

VICTORIA BELTON

God's Healing for the Rejected Soul

Copyright © Victoria Belton, 2019

All rights reserved. No part of this publication may be reproduced, distributed, or transmitted in any form or by any means, including photocopying, recording, or other electronic or mechanical methods, without the prior written permission of the publisher, except in the case of brief quotations embodied in critical reviews and certain other noncommercial uses permitted by copyright law. For permission requests, write to the publisher, addressed "Attention: Permissions Coordinator," at the address below.

Daughters of The King Ministries
www.victoriabelton.com

Quantity sales. Special discounts are available on quantity purchases by corporations, associations, and others. For details, contact the publisher at the address above.

Orders by U.S. trade bookstores and wholesalers.

ISBN-13: 9781090793515

Printed in the United States of America

ACKNOWLEDGMENTS

First and foremost, I would like to thank my Lord and Savior Jesus Christ for the gift of poetry. I pray these poems will spring forth deliverance and healing, while providing you with a bold reminder of just how much Jesus really loves you.

Pastor Rob Wallace and Pastor Katrina Wallace: WE ARE A SUCCESS.

Pastor Katrina- Thank you for the launch of *Bridging the Gap Between Vision and Reality- Making Your Dreams Come Alive*. It was what I needed to birth this book.

Elder Faye Mosby: For being a Proverbs 31 Woman. YOUR LABOR IS NOT IN VAIN. Without you putting me on blast in October 2018 announcing the book was coming soon it probably would have remained on my sun porch table neatly tucked away for just me.

Pastor Leon Steward- For calling me to confirm if I was coming to speak and you asked me, "Are you going to bring the poems you read the other day?" You know I have nothing but LOVE for you and the entire family.

Rev. Isadore Maney and Sis. Geraldine Maney for being phenomenal parents and raising me up in the church. May God continue to bless and prosper you, just as your soul prospers.

Dr. Wilma Calvert, Alyce McNeil-Boykins, and Madelon Wallace. I would like to thank each of you for listening to my poems at times when on occasion I called you.

Dr. Henry Lynn Logan- Just plain ole Thank You for believing in me and praying for increase, recording when I would go live with one of the poems on Facebook. YOU ROCK.

SECTION ONE
REJECTION OF MAN

What Have You Done?   1

The Tale of Two Dads   2

I Asked The Question?   3

No More   4

Promises, Promises, Promises   5

The 3rd Sunday Of June   6

Hatred My Escape   7

God's Way Of Escape   8

I Asked You To Come And See Me?   9

Know That I Was Not Happy   10

What Are You Looking?   12

Who Are You Looking For? Who Did You Find?   14

SECTION TWO
ABUSED BY MEN/WOMEN

World-Wide Problem 19

They Steal 20

For All The Women In The World 21

Abusers 22

You Asked Me Why I Did Not Report It 23

You Happy? I Reported It! 26

America 29

How Did This Happen? 31

How Do I Talk? 32

Some Words 33

Real Love 34

SECTION THREE
RESTORATION OF THE SOUL

There Is No Need 36

Known As 37

Be Happy 38

My Abba, Father 40

Having Me In The Palm Of Your Hand 41

What More Can I Say? 42

But God 43

So, What 44

What Are You Telling God? 46

You Pressed Forward 47

God Has Been A Father 48

God's Love 49

If Jesus 50

The Love of The Lord 51

God's Love 52

The King's Daughter 53

Send Me Your Love 54

Greater Is He 55

Other People 57

FORWARD

YOU!

YOU PLANTED THE SEED THAT SOMEONE ELSE WATERED.

YOU PLANTED THE SEED THAT SOMEONE ELSE NURTURED.

YOU PLANTED THE SEED THAT YOU DID NOT WATCH GROW!

BUT GOD HAD A RAM IN THE BUSH, TO NUTURE ME AND PROTECT ME, AND WATCH ME GROW.

DEDICATED TO MY STEP-FATHER:

REV.ISADORE MANEY

YOU DID NOT PLANT THE SEED THAT PRODUCED ME,

BUT THANK GOD YOU NUTURED ME.

YOU DID NOT PLANTED THE SEED THAT PRODUCED ME,

BUT YOU ALLOWED ME TO GROW.

YOU DID NOT PLANT THE SEED THAT PRODUCED ME,

BUT THANK GOD YOU WERE THE ONE

WHO PROTECTED ME.

SECTION 1:

REJECTION OF MAN

REJECTION
WAY LOW
ESCAPE
SELF-ESTEEM
OF ANGER
HATRED
FEAR

WHAT HAVE YOU DONE?

365 days in a year, what have you done?

12 months in a year, what have you done?

52 weeks in a calendar year, what have you done?

7 days in a week, what have you done?

Have you acknowledged me, loved me, called me?

Encouraged me, celebrated me, tolerated me?

In 365 days, what have you done?

THE TALE OF TWO DADS

One cared, and one did not.

One supported, and one did not,

One was a man, one was a boy.

One was responsible, and one was a child.

One loved, and one hated.

One stayed, and one left.

One took responsibility.

One ignored responsibility.

I ASKED THE QUESTION?

I asked the question, *what is wrong with me?*

I asked the question *why didn't you love me?*

I asked the question, *when will you love me?*

I asked the question, *what is wrong with me?*

I asked the question; *did I do something wrong?*

I asked the question, *why did you reject me?*

I asked the question, *why did you abandon me?*

I asked the question, *why did you leave me?*

NO MORE

No more waiting on you today,

no more sitting by the phone,

waiting on you to call.

No more waiting on you today,

no more sitting at the house,

waiting on you to show up.

I left before you had the opportunity

not to show up

I left because,

I'm not waiting on you **NO MORE!**

PROMISES, PROMISES, PROMISES

Promises, promises, promises!

Promises, promises, promises!

Why should I hold on to them?

You lied to me before.

and the time before that.

When the promise of having your

Father say, *"I will be there this time"*,

and he did not show up.

He promised that he would be

There *the last time*,

He promised that

He was coming the *next time*.

Promises, promises, promises.

THE 3ᴿᴰ SUNDAY OF JUNE

June 16th, 17th, 18th, 19th or 20th

Or the 3rd Sunday of every June?

Are fathers like the day it falls on?

Ever changing, unwilling to make a commitment,

undetermined to provide for their seed.

Why can't we pass the day just like any other day?

Why do we have to fake the smiles, gifts, and all the calls?

To me, it is just another plain-old ordinary day.

The 3rd Sunday in June

for the Bible,

tells us to honor our FATHER,

I will honor you,

but not celebrate you.

Who me? Celebrate Father's Day and fake the funk, laugh,

kid and smile?

NO!

HATRED MY WAY OF ESCAPE!

He did not know him not being

in my life would affect me the way it did.

For that I hated him.

He did not know that him not

loving me, would hurt me the way it did.

For that I hated him.

He did not know that him not showing up

would make me feel ashamed.

For that I hated him.

He did not know it would

embarrass me the way it did.

For that I hated him.

GOD'S WAY OF ESCAPE

Father, I forgive *him* for *him* not being in my life.

I forgive *him* for not

knowing that his absence would make my life a living nightmare.

I forgive *him* for not

protecting me, for not loving me.

I forgive him for not nurturing me.

I forgive him for not acknowledging me.

I forgive him for abandoning me.

I forgive him for rejecting me.

I forgive him for not coming to see me.

I forgive him for not celebrating my birthday.

I forgive him for not coming to celebrate *my* graduation.

I choose to forgive *him* then, now, and forever more.

I ASKED YOU TO COME AND SEE ME?

I asked you to come and see me, but you have not.

I asked you to travel the miles and distance between us,

so that we can get to know each other better.

I asked you to come and see me as a sign of how much you love me.

Prove to me that you love me be willing to travel the

distance and the miles that are between us.

Come out from your comfort zone, to my comfort zone.

I asked you to come and see me. But for what-ever reason you refused to come.

BUT EVEN IF YOU DON'T I AM OKAY WITH THAT!

KNOW THAT I WAS NOT HAPPY

KNOW THAT I WAS not happy with how things turned out with you and my mom

NO, I am not happy that you left her, or she left you, at any rate I was left alone.

Know I was left without the male figure in my life, which I so desperately needed.

Know I wanted the love of a male figure that did not want anything from me.

Know I wanted the love of a male figure who could give me the world and not want anything in return.

Know I wanted the love of a male figure who I could imagine would give me the world just because I was his little girl.

Know that I tried for years to fill the void of missing you for days, weeks, months, and years.

Now I am happy that you planted the seed that produce me, I am no longer angry that you left me.

Know now that I desire a relationship with you although things didn't turn out with you and my mom.

I want you to know I desire a relationship with you.

Know that there is just a little bit of the little girl in me that still wants to believe that her dad will desire to give her the world even if he cannot.

Know that I still desire a relationship with you, I still desire to know you and you know me.

Know that I want you to know your grandchildren.

Know that I want you to love and appreciate them.

Know that I want you to be a part of their life.

WHAT ARE YOU LOOKING FOR? WHAT DID YOU FIND?

Hey, little toddler girl!

What are you looking for?

DADA.

What did you find?

MAMA.

Hey, little preschool girl!

What are you looking for?

My Daddy.

What did you find?

My imaginary friends.

Hey, little preteen girl!

What are you looking for?

My Daddy.

What did you find?

Rejection, fear, low self-esteem, rejection, my momma anger.

Hey, teenage girl!

What are you looking for?

My Daddy.

What did you find?

Depression, my anger, insecurities.

Hey, young woman!

What are you looking for?

Looking for my Daddy.

What did you find?

My addictions: food, sex, drugs, alcohol.

My baby daddy.

Hey, adult woman!

What are you looking for?

My Daddy.

What did you find?

A father to the fatherless.

My Father, the Everlasting Father, My Abba Father.

King of Kings, Lord of Lords, Way Maker, My Savior and

Lord Jesus Christ

He was there the whole time.

Psalms 68:5

A father of the fatherless a defender of widows, is God in his holy dwelling.

WHO ARE YOU LOOKING FOR? WHO DID YOU FIND?

Hey, little toddler boy?

Who are you looking for?

DADA.

Who did you find?

MAMA.

What did you become?

A momma's baby and daddy's maybe.

Hey, preschool boy?

Who are you looking for?

My daddy.

Who did you find?

Someone my mother told me to call uncle.

What did you become?

Quiet, shy, shameful, insecure, confused

Hey, preteen boy?

Who are you looking for?

My dad, someone I can identify with,

someone that looks like me.

Someone that I

can call dad, instead of saying my uncle.

Who did you find?

Someone my mother introduces as friend

rejection, physical abuse, emotional abuse and sometimes sexual abuse

What did you become?

Fearful, shameful, embarrassed, withdrawn, and angry.

Hey, teenage boy!

Who are you looking for?

My dad.

Who did you find?

My gang buddies

My anger

my mother being hurt

by the man she told me to call her friend.

Fear, rejection and trouble in the streets.

What did you become? – Angry, fearful, rebellious, insecure, depressed, an alcoholic, a drug addict, suicidal.

Hey, young man!

Who are you looking for?

My dad.

Who did you find?

My baby momma, my parole officer.

What did you become?

Selfish, prideful, lover of myself, lonely, womanizer.

Hey, adult man?

Who are you looking for?

My dad?

Who did you find?

THE ABBA FATHER, THE EVERLASTING FATHER, THE KING OF KINGS, AND THE LORD OF LORDS, MY LORD AND SAVIOR, JESUS CHRIST.

WHO DID YOU BECOME?

A MIGHTY MAN OF VALOR, A FAITHFUL SERVENT, A MAN OF INTERGRITY, A WORSHIPPER, A FRIEND OF GOD

Judges 6:12

And the angel of the LORD appeared unto him, and said unto him, The LORD *is* with thee, thou mighty man of valour.

SECTION TWO:
ABUSE OF MEN/WOMEN
REJECTION OF SELF

ABUSE
MISCONDUCT
TORTURE
SEXUAL
TORMENT

WORLD-WIDE PROBLEM

This is a world-wide problem.

Sexual abuse in the family, in the work place,

and in the Bible.

It's an age-old problem.

Not just in the USA,

Worldwide

It covers all the seven

Continents,

Africa, Antarctica,

Asia, Australia,

Europe, North America,

and South America.

This is a world-wide problem.

If my people, which are called by my name.
Shall humble themselves and pray, and seek my face, and turn from their wicked ways then will I hear from heaven and forgive their sin, and will heal their land.
2 Chronicles 7:14 (KJV)

THEY STEAL

They steal your innocence.

They steal your self-worth.

They steal your virginity.

They rob you of your joy, peace,

virtue, honor, and dignity.

Each time they lay

with you, they steal.

The enemy come to steal, kill and destroyed.

God, you replace my innocence.

God, you replace my peace, my joy.

God, you replace my virtue, my honor, and my dignity.

You remold me.

You make me into my original form.

The thief comes only in order to steal, kill and destroy.
I have come in order that you might have life- life in all its
fullness. John 10:10
(GNT)

FOR ALL THE WOMEN IN THE WORLD

For all the women in the world,

Whether you are a black or white woman.

Asian women or Spanish women.

For all the women in the world,

That uncle touches your breast,

put their hand between your thighs,

For all the women in the world

that brother, cousin, or your mom's friends

that lay with you.

Know you are better than that.

Know that Jesus loves you and HE will see you

through all the hurt, pain and shame.

ABUSERS

Abusers come in all different sizes and shapes.

Abusers come short and tall,

Abusers come skinny and fat.

Abusers come in all different shades of color.

Abusers come in all colors, races, creed, religions.

Abusers come with long hair and short hair,

Abusers come, and they go.

Abusers hurt and steal.

Abusers steal your self-worth,

Abusers steal your joy.

Abusers steal your peace,

Abusers steal your identity.

Abusers come, they hurt, they steal then

they go to their next victim.

They may have stolen your past,

don't let them steal your future.

YOU ASKED ME WHY I DID NOT REPORT IT!

YOU ASKED ME WHY I DID NOT REPORT IT AT 5?

How does a 5-year-old talk about something that the violator, predator, abuser did? How does a 5-year report something that happen to them by a person they trusted? How does a five-year-old talk about what the abuser said to keep silent? How does a 5-year-old report something that is supposedly everybody is doing? How does a 5-year-old know that the feeling in their gut is their body letting their mind know that something is wrong?

YOU ASKED ME WHY I DID NOT REPORT IT AT 10?

Who would believe that a 10-year-old was being violated by an uncle, uncle friend, a brother's friend, family friend, dad, step dad, aunt, cousin, sister, mother, cousin, grandfather, mother friend? Why did someone not notice the difference? Why did someone not pick up, that the excessive chattiness in our conversation was a way for us to express my anxiety, fear, frustrations? Who would believe that this happens in my race? We don't do that type of thing. Other people do that? They are disgusting.

YOU ASKED ME WHY I DID NOT REPORT IT AT 15?

Who would not tell me that it was just boys being boys? Who would support me? Who would not blame me? Who would stand up for me? Maybe I did not report it because I buried the emotion that is attached to my pain? I silenced the voices in my head that is trying to make me remember the past? Who would believe that a man could be raped or violated? Who would believe that a man of God would hurt me? Who would believe that it was not an honor or privilege to work side by side with them?

YOU ASKED ME WHY I DID NOT REPORT IT AT 20?

Who would believe that the abuse was buried so deep in my spirit that the memory of the abuse become so suppressed that I became paralyze? Who would tell me that I just have to accept it? It's happen to most people. Maybe I thought that if I was promiscuous it would put the ball in my court. Who would tell me not just shut down and be quieted?

YOU ASKED ME WHY I DID NOT REPORT IT AT 25?

Who would not judge me and say I should have been at home before noon? Who would not say I should have worn a longer skirt? Who would not just have accused me of being just drunk, too loose or asking for it? Maybe I thought to myself how this happened again to me. Lord what did I do to deserve this?

YOU ASKED ME WHY I DID NOT REPORT IT AT 30?

You would believe his word against mine. Who would stand up and say this is wrong? It's the normal not the abnormal. It's to be expected, live with it! I had too. How do you know I did not report it? I did not have to report it they already knew and did not want to report the abuser? Maybe the pain of their past hinders them from acting on my pain. They become frozen once again.

YOU ASKED ME WHY I DID NOT REPORT IT AT 35?

Maybe I thought if I am a great employee the boss would just leave me alone and not harass me. Feel on me or grope me. Maybe if I wore a blouse buttoned up to my neck in the middle of the July my boss would not bother me? Maybe I did not report it because by the time I realize what had happened it was too late.

He was cunning with his subtle moves yet sudden moves. Does that make sense to you? Do you understand what I am saying? **OH SILLY ME.**

HOW COULD I NOT RECOGNIZE THIS UNTIL IT WAS TOO LATE.

I REPORTED IT: I am reclaiming my body, my dignity. I am reclaiming the fact that no one has the right to touch me or violate me. I am not responsible for this. I refused to suffer in silence, guilt or shame any longer. I finally got my strength and courage. I finally decided to tell my story. No matter if people believed me or not.

NO, I DID NOT REPORT IT AT 5, 10, 15, 20, 25 30,35.

I REPORTED IT AT 40! WHAT'S YOUR STANCE?

YOU HAPPY? I REPORTED I!

I reported it and they put me on trial.

I reported it and they called me a lie.

I reported it and they said that I was too loose,

they said that I took too long to report it.

I reported it, and no one still believe me.

I reported it and I was mocked and made fun of.

I reported it and the law officers did not do anything to make it better.

You happy now, that I reported it.

It was better when I kept my mouth shut according to some people.

I was from the wrong side of the tracks for them to believe me.

I should have taken it my grave.

I reported it now what are going to do?

Blame me, shame me again,

try to silence me again. By telling me I should have stayed silence.

I reported it and I became a victim all over again.

You happy now, I reported it and they mocked me

and made fun of me all over again.

I had to remember everything and tell you everything I remember.

I had to bring all the memories and emotions back up that I tried to hide for so long.

You happy now, I reported it and I am still the one to blame. I reported it as a victim, but I am still being victimized and terrorized about something that the law, the justice system said I should report.

You happy now, I reported it and they asked for a witness. Who commits a crime with someone knowingly watching?

You happy now, I reported it and the justice system did not do anything.

You happy now, I reported it and they barely questioned him.

I know that LADY LIBERTY IS BLIND, but I did not think she was blind, deaf, and cripple.

LADY LIBERTY CANNOT SEE THE PAIN AND DISTRESS.

LADY LIBERTY CANNOT HEAR THE VICTIMS, MALE AND FEMALE CRYING THE SILENT TEARS DOWN THROUGH THE YEARS.

LADY LIBERTY CANNOT WALK THE PATH THAT THE VICTIM HAS WALKED

But I guess when you have a blind fold on over your eyes you cannot be anything but blind. But the lawyer's, prosecutors as well as the district attorney don't have blind folds on, neither do the people over them.

I REPORTED IT **YOU HAPPY.**

AMERICA

AMERICA is worried about protecting the boys from being falsely accused. When some of them have been silently abused.

AMERICA who is protecting the boys from the women?

AMERICA who is protecting the boys from the men.

AMERICA who is protecting the boys from the boys. You talk about the women not reporting.

AMERICA the boys and men are victims too. Oh, don't just say that is not the truth: that this is all so taboo.

AMERICA did you just think it was only happening to girls and women, not boys and men?

AMERICA you see boys are victims of abuse too. They just don't report it either.

AMERICA, they live with the shame, guilt, and pain. Some become quiet, shy and introverted and some become loud, angry and extroverted. Some become abusers of boys and men. While others abuse girls and become users of women. They date women by the dozens to hide their pain, that's a game. They think they enjoy playing the dating game to throw you off course. Some become abusers of drugs and alcohol or both.

AMERICA many are too ashamed to admit that a portion of their manhood has been stripped away from them. Too afraid to admit their innocence is gone. Too afraid to admit they could not defend themselves.

AMERICA, Well I have a question for you it is an old age one? Did they report, and did you turn a deaf ear?

AMERICA, did you shut your mind down and refused to listen? Did you close your eyes as if you could not see?   It does not dismiss their story. They keep silent. **AMERICA**

HOW DID THIS HAPPEN

How did this happen?

Emotional abuse.

It starts subtle.

Then it escalates.

Day by day.

Insult by insult.

They gnaw, bite

and chew away at you

until it's nothing left.

You are a hole, empty, void without any feeling or thoughts.

Feeling bad about what you did not do or

feeling bad about what you did do,

The decision you made or did not make.

You are just left empty.

HOW DO I TALK?

How do I talk about all the pain inside?

The stuff that I have taken with stride?

How do I talk about all the pain inside?

All the mistakes that I have made?

How do I express pain that cannot be expressed?

Do I just repress it, or do I just bury it?

Because I cannot express the pain.

SOME WORDS

Some words are taken for granted,

Some words are taken to heart.

Some words hurt, cut and bruise.

Some words torment.

Some words bring joy, love and peace.

Rather the word is good or bad,

It will have a lasting effect.

So, choose your words wisely,

For one day you will be judged,

For your words rather good or bad.

I can guarantee that on judgment day people will have to give an account of every careless word they say.
Matthew 12:36 (GWT)

REAL LOVE

Real love is true...not fake or phony.

Real love is kind...not cruel and does not criticize.

Real love is joy...not sadness or grief.

Real love is patience...not jealous or mean.

Real love is gentle...not hard or rough.

Real love does not hurt, kick or punch you.

It's love...it cannot do such a thing.

Love is patient and kind; it is not jealous or conceited or proud;
Love is not ill mannered or selfish or irritable;
love does not keep a record or wrongs;
love is not happy with evil but is happy with truth.
Love never gives up; and its faith,
hope, and patience never fail.
1 Corinthians 13:4-7

SECTION THREE

MOVING FORWARD

FATHER COVERED
HAPPINESS BY
RESTORATION
THE OF CHILD
LOVE THE LOVE SELF-LOVE
MOVING
FATHER'S LOVE
FORWARD KING LOVE
GOD'S THE BLOOD
ABBA HEALING

THERE IS NO NEED

There is no need in feeling blue,

Jesus has already delivered you!

Just when you thought all hope

Was gone,

Just when you thought no end

Was in sight.

He suddenly made you strong.

Jesus rescued you with all His might.

KNOWN AS

Known as the bastard child from this world point of view,

Known as the fatherless child from my point of view.

Known as *momma baby and daddy's maybe* from

My mom 's point of view.

But from God's point of view, I am known as the King's CHILD

I am known as the KING'S CHILD from God's point of view.

**I will be your father, and you shall be my sons
and daughters, says the Lord Almighty.
2 Corinthians 6:18 (GNT)**

BE HAPPY

BE HAPPY WITH YOURSELF!

SHORT/TALL,

BIG OR SMALL FRAME.

DARK SKIN, LIGHT SKIN

MOCHA SKIN, COCOA SKIN

NAPPY HAIR, PROCESS HAIR,

TWIST HAIR, WEAVE HAIR,

NO HAIR, STRAIGHT HAIR, WAVY HAIR

BLUE EYES, BROWN EYES,

HAZEL EYES.

GLASSES ON/GLASSES OFF. CONTACTS IN,

CONTACTS OFF.

BUCKED TEETH. NO TEETH.

CRACKED TEETH. CROOKED TEETH.

BE HAPPY WITH YOUR APPEARANCE.

YOU ARE WHO GOD CREATED YOU TO BE!

YOU ARE FEARFULLY AND WONDERFULLY MADE.

YOU WERE CREATED PERFECTLY

ACCORDING TO THE MASTER PLAN.

I will praise You because I have been remarkably and wonderfully made. Your works are wonderful, and I know this well.
Psalm 139:14 (HCSB)

MY ABBA, FATHER

My Abba, Father

You are my Abba Father,

my source and sustainer.

You are my Abba Father,

my strength and my redeemer.

You are my Abba Father,

my joy and peace.

For ye have not received the spirit of bondage again to fear; but ye have received the Spirit of adoption, whereby we cry, Abba, Father. Romans 8:15 (KJV)

HAVING ME IN THE PALM OF YOUR HAND

Lord, thank You for having me in the palm of your hand.

Even when I did not know the plan.

Thank You planting my feet on solid ground.

Thank You for having me in Your plan when I could not see my way.

You carried me every step of the way, each place

that I journeyed.

Each person that I met, whether for a season, event, or lifetime.

For I know the thoughts that I think toward you, saith the LORD, thoughts of peace, and not of evil, to give you an expected end.
Jeremiah 29:11 (KJV)

WHAT MORE CAN I SAY?

What more can I say,

But, *Thank You God!*

You are a Healer!

What more can I say,

But, *Thank You, God.*

You have healed me.

What more can I say,

But Thank You, God,

I am healed!

He said, "If you listen carefully to the LORD your God and do what is right in his eyes, if you pay attention to his commands and keep all his decrees, I will not bring on you any of the diseases I brought on the Egyptians, for I am the LORD, who heals you."

Exodus 15:26 (GWT)

BUT GOD

Some men will try to destroy you,

But God.

Some men will reject you,

But God.

Some men will hate you,

But God.

Some men will speak all manner of evil against you,

But God.

No weapon formed against me shall prosper

Isaiah 54:17

SO, WHAT

So, what you slept with that married man?

You are not an adulterer any more.

So, what you had sex outside of marriage?

You are no longer a fornicator now.

So, what you used to get drunk?

You are sober now.

So, what you used to steal?

You are honest now.

So, what you used to lie?

You tell the truth now.

So, what you used to walk in unforgiveness?

You walk in forgiveness now.

So, what you had a carnal mind?

You have the mind of Christ now.

Satan is an accuser of the brethren.

He loves to remind you of your past.

Don't listen to him.

Whom the Son sets free, is free indeed.

If the Son therefore shall make you free,
ye shall be free indeed. (KJV)
John 8:36

WHAT ARE YOU TELLING GOD?

Are you telling God that He made a mistake?

Every time you look in the mirror?

Are you mumbling and complaining?

My nose is flat, my eyes are too small, my teeth are too big

or my face is too wide?

Are you mumbling and complaining *my lips are too thin?*

My lips are too wide, my legs are too skinny?

The Creator of the universe does not want to hear that.

The Creator of the universe made *you*!

You are His craftsmanship.

For we are his workmanship,

created in Christ Jesus unto good works,

which God hath before ordained

that we should walk in them.

Ephesians 2:10   (KJV)

YOU PRESSED FORWARD

YOU PRESSED FORWARD.

EVEN WITH FEAR, SHAME AND DISGRACE.

YOU DID NOT STAY

IN THE SAME PLACE.

YOU PUSH, YOU PRAYED,

YOU TREVAIL AND MOVE FORWARD.

FORGETTING THE PAST.

YOU PRESSED FORWARD.

EVEN WITH FEAR, SHAME AND DISGRACE.

YOU DID NOT STAY

IN THE SAME PLACE.

YOU PUSHED, YOU PRAYED,

YOU TREVAIL AND MOVED FORWARD,

FORGETTING THE PAST.

Brethen, I do not regard myself as having laid hold of it yet: but one thing I do: forgetting what lies behind and reaching forward to what lies ahead. **Phil 3:13 (NASB)**

GOD HAS BEEN A FATHER!

God has been a Father to me.

He has held me close.

His love won't disappear.

His love does not add anger or fear.

His love just adds love and good cheer.

GOD'S LOVE

God's love is not a temporary

feeling or fix.

His love is never ending and does not quit.

His love is everlasting and eternal.

There is nothing you can do to earn it,

God's love is available to all.

God's love is free from

Lies, hurt, abuse and shame.

God's love is truth, pain free and joyous.

IF JESUS

If Jesus set me free

Why should I be bound?

Free from all guilt

and shame.

That old stuff can't remain.

Because I am not the same!

As far as the east is from the west,
so far does he remove our sins from us.
Psalm 103:12 (GNT)

THE LOVE OF THE LORD

THE LOVE OF THE LORD

SURROUNDS ME EACH AND EVERY DAY.

THE LOVE OF GOD FLOWS CONTINUOUSLY THROUGHOUT THE DAY.

THE LOVE OF GOD COVERS ME 365 DAYS OF THE YEAR.

THE LOVE OF GOD LASTS 24 HOURS A DAY, 7 DAYS A WEEK.

THE LOVE OF GOD DOES NOT STOP FOR THE HOLIDAY.

THE LOVE OF GOD DOES NOT GET MAD OR QUIT.

THE LOVE OF GOD DOES NOT FILL YOU WITH GUILT.

THE LOVE OF GOD GIVES YOU AN ATTITUDE OF GRATITUDE.

Love is patient. Love is kind. Love isn't jealous. It doesn't sing its own praises. It isn't arrogant.
It isn't rude. It doesn't think about itself. It isn't irritable. It doesn't keep track of wrongs.
It isn't happy when injustice is done, but it is happy with the truth. Love never gives up; and its faith, hope, and patience never fail. *1*
Corinthians 13: 4-7

GOD'S LOVE

I was astonished to know that God loved me.

That He made and fashioned me.

I was shocked to know that God loved me,

Amazed to know that He cared for me.

Oh, what an amazing love that God has for me.

I am a work of fine art in His eyesight,

A precious jewel that is well pleasing in His sight,

A perfect delight.

Keep me as the apple of YOUR eye, hide me under the shadow of your almighty wing.

Keep me as the apple of the eye, Hide me under the shadow of thy wings.
Psalm 17:8 (KJV)

THE KINGS DAUGHTER

DAUGHTER OF THE KING

YOU REIGN SUPREME.

DAUGHTER OF THE KING,

YOU HAVE PEACE WITHIN.

DAUGHTER OF THE KING

YOU HAVE LOVE WITHIN.

YOU HAVE STRENGTH AND

INNER BEAUTY.

THE KING'S DAUGHTER IS FREE.

THE KING'S DAUGHTER IS LOVE.

THE KING'S DAUGHTER IS ACCEPTED,

NOT JUST TOLERATED.

SEND ME YOUR LOVE

OH LORD, PLEASE SEND ME YOUR LOVE.

YOUR LOVE IS UNDENIABLE!

YOUR PEACE IS UNSPEAKABLE!

YOUR JOY IS UNCONCEIVEABLE!

AS I START A NEW LIFE,

AS OF NOW I START TO CELEBRATE MY LIFE IN CHRIST,

I START TO LIVE A FULL LIFE OF JOY, PEACE,

HOPE AND LOVE.

GREATER IS HE!

Greater is HE that is in me than HE that is in the world.

Greater is the love that is in me than the hate that is in the world.

Greater is the joy that is in my than the depression that Satan tries to put on me.

Greater is the salvation that is in me- than the sin that is ever lurking to find me.

Greater is the peace that God has bestowed upon me that the anxiety that is trying to take me over.

Greater is the faith that is in me-than that fear that has tried to keep me fearful.

Greater is the steadfastness in me than the shackles that they to stop me.

Greater is the renewed mind that is in me that the old corrupted mind that was once

within me.

Greater is the vision that is in me that the devil that is trying to distract me.

Greater is the blood of Jesus that is running through my veins them the generational

Curses that think they can remain.

1 John 4:4

Ye are of God, little children, and have overcome them: because greater is he that is in you, than he that is in the world.

OTHER PEOPLE

Other people may reject you, but I don't want you to reject you.

Other people may put you down, but I don't want you to put you down.

Other people may give up on you, but I don't want you to give up on you.

Other people may call you ugly, but I don't want you to call yourself ugly.

Other people may talk bad about you, but I don't want you to talk bad about you.

Other people may not see your worth, but I don't want you not to see your worth.

Other people may think negative thoughts about you, but I don't want you to think negative thoughts about you.

Start believing in the fact the you are fearfully and wonderfully made.

Start believing that you are special.

Start believing you are worthy of life.

Don't reject you.

Just because other people reject *you.*

LOVE YOURSELF.

EMBRACE YOURSELF.

Love and embrace yourself Daughter of the King.

Love and embrace yourself Son of the King.

Love and embrace yourself Child of the King.

God will never reject you.

HE RESTORED MY SOUL

PSALM 23:3 HE RESTORED MY SOUL....

I looked up and I was restored.

He restored my soul.

He replenished my spirit.

He renewed my mind.

Psalms 23:3

He restoreth my soul: he leadeth me in the paths of righteousness for his name's sake. (KJV)

ABOUT THE AUTHOR

Elder Victoria Belton is a native of St. Louis, Mo. She was called to ministry in 2000 and baptized in Jesus' Name in 2001. She served in her father's church for many years, organizing programs, teaching Sunday school, and singing in the choir. She believes in the power of prayer. This is her first published book.

She has a strong desire to see people healed, delivered, and set free in Jesus name. She is the overseer for Daughter of the King Ministries. She ministers women who suffer with a spirit of rejection, abandonment, sexual and emotional abuse.

She is a member of Peace of Faith Church under the leadership of Pastor Robert Wallace and Pastor Katrina Wallace.

For more information about Elder Victoria or to contact her you may visit her website victoriabelton.com

Made in the
USA
Middletown, DE